DONCASTER'S RAILWAYS

D1612922

John Law

AMBERLEY

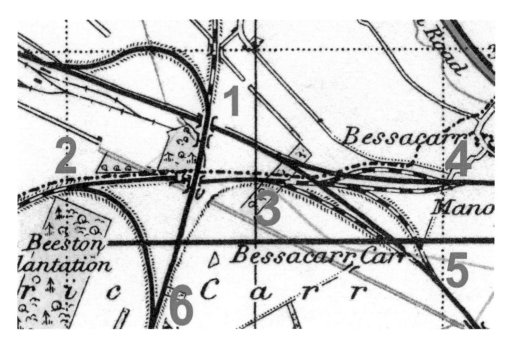

The Railways Around the Black Carr Area

Adopted from the 1 inch Ordnance Survey map, dated 1947.

1. Low Ellers Junction
2. Black Carr Sidings West
3. Black Carr Sidings East
4. Bessacarr Junction
5. Loversall Carr Junction
6. St Catherines Junction

First published 2017

Amberley Publishing
The Hill, Stroud
Gloucestershire, GL5 4EP

www.amberley-books.com

Copyright © John Law, 2017

The right of John Law to be identified as
the Author of this work has been asserted in
accordance with the Copyrights, Designs and
Patents Act 1988.

ISBN 978 1 4456 5946 6 (print)
ISBN 978 1 4456 5947 3 (ebook)

British Library Cataloguing in Publication Data.
A catalogue record for this book is available from
the British Library.

Typesetting by Amberley Publishing.
Printed in the UK.

Introduction

Doncaster, South Yorkshire, can trace its history back to Roman times, when a fort called Danum was built on what was to become the Great North Road. Gradually the town grew to become a regional centre with an important market. The coming of the railways brought much prosperity to Doncaster, especially after the decision was made by the Great Northern Railway to move the company's main works to a site between the station and the River Don.

The opening of the South Yorkshire Railway, soon followed by other lines, saw Doncaster becoming a major junction, with routes radiating out to all points of the compass. Pre-Grouping days at Doncaster must have produced a fascinating scene, with trains from the Great Northern, Great Eastern, North Eastern, Great Central, Midland and Lancashire & Yorkshire Railways.

The expansion eastwards of the South Yorkshire coalfield saw many new collieries being opened around the beginning of the twentieth century, with various railway lines being constructed to serve them. All this extra traffic meant that Doncaster station became very congested, giving an incentive for alternative routes like the Dearne Valley Railway and the various joint lines. The railway map of the area in the 1920s was very confusing!

The well-documented end of steam on British Railways occurred in 1968, but this took place effectively a year earlier in the Doncaster area, fifty years ago, making it a good starting point for this publication. Doncaster station has seen many changes since then, with green locomotives and diesel multiple units being given a coat of corporate British Rail blue, all to be later replaced by more modern motive power.

Perhaps the most important development of the period came in 1979, when Doncaster Power Signal Box opened, replacing North and South cabins and all the mechanical boxes in the surrounding area. The track layout in the station was completely changed, with all through platforms becoming bi-directional, giving more flexibility at times of disruption. More recent work to relieve congestion has been the construction of Platform 0 and the redoubling of the curve to the Sheffield line.

The end of Class 55 'Deltics' on East Coast Main Line duties in the early 1980s brought in the era of the InterCity 125 high speed trains; however, most of these were transferred to other routes when the ECML was electrified in the later years of that decade.

Doncaster Works, always known locally as the 'Plant', still performed an important role in the post-steam era. The last locomotives constructed included part of the Class 56 fleet and the Class 58 locomotives, the latter ending production in 1987.

The overhauling of locomotives continued, but gradually the Plant's role became less important and the inevitable occurred in 2007, when much of the works closed and the famous Crimpsall shop was demolished. Nevertheless, plenty of refurbishment work is still undertaken in the old carriage and wagon shop area by Wabtec Limited, whose operations can often be viewed from the station.

South of Doncaster station, Doncaster 'Carr Loco' steam shed continued in use, gradually becoming smaller as demand receded, and finally closing under DB Schenker ownership in 2014. At the time of writing, the depot for maintenance of the new generation of trains on the East Coast Main Line is under construction. Decoy and Belmont yards are still busy, especially with the construction of the new Railport. The complex junctions to the south were considerably remodelled in the late 1970s. Today passenger trains often use the Dearne Valley flyover, on a line that was built solely for mineral traffic.

North of Doncaster, new stations have been built at Bentley and Adwick on the electrified line towards Wakefield and Leeds. Perhaps the most important project was the construction of a new link, including a viaduct from the Stainforth–Adwick line, over the ECML, to the Askern route, reducing heavy freight over the busy line towards York. Regarding the Askern line, passenger trains have been reintroduced, with Grand Central running their black trains through to Pontefract and beyond.

Another new station was opened at Kirk Sandall, to some degree replacing the closed facility at nearby Barnby Dun. Sadly the last coal mine in the area, Hatfield Colliery, closed in 2015. Coal traffic still survives, for the moment, imported via Immingham, passing through the area destined for the Aire Valley power stations. A newer development has been the importation of biomass fuel, following the same route.

Closure of the local mines has meant the disappearance of the branches to serve them, including the Dearne Valley Railway, the Hull & Barnsley's Denaby branch and the H&B and Great Central Joint. Surprisingly the former South Yorkshire Joint Railway is still in operation and sees considerable freight traffic, despite the demolition of all its collieries.

What will become of Doncaster's railways in the future? The current InterCity 225 sets will be replaced by the new Japanese-designed Azuma trains, built in County Durham, but to be maintained at Doncaster. At the time of writing, freight traffic is in decline but, with the expansion of the Railport, the opposite may apply in the Doncaster area. Passenger traffic seems to be increasing throughout the country so there may be other developments on the local railways of South Yorkshire. Maybe a decent direct service to Lincoln serving Robin Hood Airport or a new station at Askern with an hourly service to Pontefract? Who knows? We live in interesting times!

Finally, my thanks to Bob Ashton, Jim Sambrooks, the late Les Flint and Alan Walker for providing a few photographs and to Keith Evison for driving me to a couple of places off the beaten track by public transport.

Doncaster Station and its Environs

Despite this book concentrating on Doncaster's railways after the demise of steam, the first photograph we see is that of preserved Great Western Railway 4-6-0 No. 7029 *Clun Castle*. Heading an Ian Allan special to Leeds, it has stopped on the Down fast line in Doncaster station for a crew change on 17 September 1967. The driver of the 350-hp diesel shunter (and match wagon) is having a good look at this unusual sight, but few enthusiasts are around to record the event. It is interesting to note that the water column is still in place, though the loco had been filled up earlier in Peterborough and was not required on this occasion.

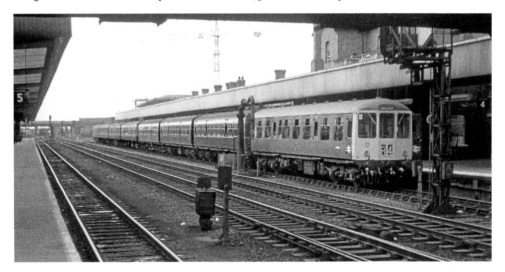

It is mid-1967 and British Rail's blue livery is beginning to make an appearance, albeit only on one vehicle of this eight-car mixed formation diesel multiple unit (DMU), which has just arrived and terminated in Doncaster station's Platform 4. The leading car was built by the Birmingham Railway Carriage and Wagon Works, while Metro-Cammell constructed the following three. The rearmost four-car set appears to be a Derby-built unit. The blue square, seen on the lower left front of the first carriage, indicates that it can be worked in multiple with any other unit bearing the same symbol. The tower crane, seen in the background, is being used in the construction of the multi-storey car park over the Northern bus station. Thanks to Alan Walker for taking this photograph.

Once it was constructed, the multi-storey car park over the Doncaster's Northern bus station provided a great place to photograph the north end of the railway station and its approaches. Looking down, *circa* 1968, we see Brush type diesel number D1547 on a northbound express. The loco is newly painted in BR corporate livery, as are its carriages, while other items of rolling stock are still in green, including the Metro-Cammell DMU car behind Doncaster C signal box. The more modern Doncaster North signal box is to the right. Other items of interest include the Works offices in the background, while cattle pens are still *in situ* in the left foreground. Finally, a 350-hp diesel shunter leaves Platform 1 with its match wagon.

Many East Coast Main Line expresses were hauled by English Electric Type 5 'Deltic' locomotives, later to become Class 55. D9004 is such an example. Looking smart in its blue colours, it is named *Queen's Own Highlander*, as it departs northwards out of Doncaster with a rake of early Mk II carriages, some time in 1969.

The year 1969 was very much a transitional period for British Rail's livery scheme. In the west carriage sidings behind Doncaster station is Brush Type 4 No. 1980 (still carrying its obsolete 'D' prefix). It remains in its two-tone green colours, while the Mk I rolling stock is in blue and grey. The locomotive entered traffic in 1965, became No. 47278 in 1974, and was finally withdrawn in 2000.

After the 1947 resignalling, Doncaster station was controlled by two modern power signal boxes, at the north and south ends. On 1 May 1968, Doncaster South signal box is seen, photographed from the end of Platform 4. Closure came on 8 July 1979, when the new signalling centre (almost opposite South box) opened.

The year 1975 saw British Rail begin a DMU refurbishment programme, with those that had undergone the process receiving a pleasant white-based colour scheme. Newly painted in that livery is a four-car Derby-built set, seen at Platform 4 in 1977, having just terminated.

Another refurbished DMU, this time built by Metro-Cammell, is arriving in Doncaster's Platform 4 in 1978 on a service to Sheffield and Manchester. Clearly seen on the left is the Doncaster North signal box, with only a year of existence to go. The building on the right housed the station announcer, who had a grand view of events throughout the station.

As a DMU sits in south-facing bay Platform 2, 350-hp diesel shunter No. 08881 moves some cement wagons through Platform 4 *c.* 1978. In front of the locomotive is a match truck, the sole purpose of which was to assist in the operation of track circuits, particularly on little-used sections of line.

Entering service as D1506 in 1963, No. 47407 was allocated to Finsbury Park when this photograph was taken *c.* 1977. The loco is in charge of an Up Pullman express as it passes through Doncaster, watched carefully by the track worker and a couple of train spotters on Platform 4. No. 47407 was withdrawn in 1990 and cut up at Frodingham in 1995.

Until their withdrawal in the early 1980s, the Class 55 Deltics were a familiar sight in Doncaster station, hauling the East Coast Main Line expresses from King's Cross to the north. In Platform 5 in 1978, No. 55012 *Crepello* is in charge of a Down train of BR Mk II carriages, including the High Speed Track Recording Coach directly behind the loco. The HSTRC, as it was widely known, was the bane of permanent way engineers' lives as it was prone to discovering a whole series of minor track faults as it ran over the network. Each one had to be prioritised and dealt with.

We have already seen Doncaster North and South signal boxes within these pages. In 1947 they replaced the original Great Northern Railway mechanical signalling, but one reminder of those days was 'C' Box, which was left in place to control the goods lines around the back of Platform 8. Here it is *c.* 1977. It would be demolished in 1979, when the whole station trackwork was re-modelled and new multiple-aspect signalling introduced.

Sunday 8 July 1979 saw the Doncaster station area come under the control of the new Doncaster Power Signal Box. The station area itself was remodelled, as was Marshgate Junction, just to the north. Here is the new layout in autumn 1980, with an Up High Speed Train passing through. The Leeds line diverges to the left, while the route to Hull and Cleethorpes curves sharply to the right. The Doncaster Avoiding Line, built by the Great Central Railway in 1910, can be seen on the embankment and bridges in the background.

The 1979 resignalling saw some platforms re-numbered within Doncaster station. One south-facing bay was removed, so Platform 4 became number 3. That facility was also lengthened and divided into two sections. Standing at Platform 3B (the north end) in 1979 is an ex-Western Region Class 123 DMU, the leading car being E52096. As the train is heading for Sheffield, it will use a series of crossovers to reach the single lead junction to access the former GCR route.

The ubiquitous Brush Type 4 diesel locomotive, later known as the Class 47, was used for a variety of roles in the Doncaster area. In autumn 1980, No. 47373 approaches the station with a well-laden southbound 'merry-go-round' train of coal, probably heading for one of the Nottinghamshire power stations. Straddling the layout in the background is the town's North Bridge, built in 1910, when it replaced a most inconvenient level crossing.

In September 1980, alongside a DMU at Platform 6, is No. 47052, awaiting its next duty in the middle road siding. The locomotive, new as D1634 in 1964, was allocated to Immingham at the time of being photographed, but was soon transferred to York. It was later to receive Freightliner livery and was finally scrapped in 2003. The first car of the DMU, E50297, was built by Craven's of Sheffield and is the driving motor brake second of a two-car set.

Sometime around 1981, a lengthy Up Freightliner container train is passing through Doncaster station on the fast lines behind an unidentified Class 47. Standing in platform 3B is a Derby-built DMU, one of many used on local services in and around South Yorkshire.

Doncaster does not generally suffer from extremes of weather, thanks to its proximity to sea level and the fact that the foothills of the Pennines to the west shelter the town. However, the winter of 1981 brought a covering of snow, sufficient to cause a degree of inconvenience to rail travellers. In this photograph, only the platform lines have seen traffic, as an Up HST sits in Platform 3A before departing for King's Cross.

Seen from the vantage point of the multi-storey cark park over Doncaster's Northern bus station is a view over the main line, and part of the complex of sidings serving Doncaster Works, in autumn 1980. As a Derby-built two-car DMU heads north out of the station, a Class 08 350-hp diesel shunter shunts a pair MGR hoppers around the wagon works yard. Behind it are some newly painted parcels vans. In the right background are several DMU cars awaiting entry to, or collection from, the DMU Shop.

A block of flats, named Cusworth House, is the location for another 1980 aerial view of Doncaster Works frontage, this time to the south of the station. An unidentified Class 46 diesel has just left the station with an Up train of BR Mk I stock. It has just gained the Up fast line as it passes a Class 55 Deltic on standby duties. In the foreground is what was once Doncaster Central goods depot.

The first thirty Class 56 locomotives were built for British Rail in Romania, but No. 56032 is a true Doncaster locomotive. Outshopped from the 'Plant' (always the unofficial name for Doncaster Works) in 1977, the locomotive is seen around the back of Doncaster station with an Up train of HAA merry-go-round wagons, in May 1981. No doubt it will be heading for one of the local collieries for reloading.

Two green celebrities in the same picture. Deltic No. 55002 *King's Own Yorkshire Light Infantry* is stopped by the signal outside Doncaster station on the 05.50 from King's Cross in May 1981. It is waiting for No. 40106 on the newspaper empties to Red Bank, Manchester, which is taking the single-lead junction onto the Sheffield line. Happily, both locos have since been preserved. Between the two trains, the remains of one of the platforms of St James' Bridge excursion station can be seen. The ugly grey concrete building was Doncaster Cold Stores, with the suburb of Hexthorpe (built to house workers in the Plant) beyond.

The second day of 1982 saw the end of an era on British Rail, as the final day of the Deltics. No. 55015 *Tulyar* was in charge of the 'Deltic Scotsman Farewell' railtour, seen leaving Doncaster on its northbound journey at 10.42, about ten minutes behind schedule. It arrived in Edinburgh only three minutes late. Behind the former Great Northern Railway water tower is Crimpsall Ings power station, itself now history, as Doncaster Prison has been built on its site.

British Rail's corporate blue livery is well illustrated here on this short convoy of locomotives bypassing Doncaster station in mid-1983. Sulzer Type 4 No. 45013 leads Brush Type 2 locos Nos 31198 and 31178 southwards, probably to Carr traction maintenance depot, less than a mile away. No. 45013 remained in service until 1987, being scrapped in 1994. No. 31198 suffered the same fate in 1991, while No. 31178 lasted until 2000, having completed forty years' service.

The Brush Type 2 locomotives, later known as Class 31s, were a common sight around Doncaster on less heavy-duty rosters. On such a working, with just two parcels vans is No. 31428, named *The North Yorkshire Moors Railway*, between Platforms 6 and 7 in May 1988. It had been new in 1960 as D5635, but it later became No. 31211 and was renumbered as 31428 in 1983. It was finally withdrawn for scrapping in 2001.

In mid-1986, prior to electrification, grey-liveried No. 31296 takes advantage of the bi-directional working through Platform 4 at Doncaster station, as it heads south with a *very* short load. The hopper wagon being towed belongs to British Industrial Sand, so one assumes that it is heading for repair, having been removed from the glassmaking facility near Barnby Dun. The locomotive had previously been numbered D5829, having been delivered to British Railways in 1965.

The English Electric Type 4 diesel locomotives were introduced to British Railways metals in 1958, with deliveries continuing until 1962. When new, they were allocated to express duties but, towards the end of their lives, they were relegated to less prestigious workings. In spring 1984, No. 40086 (new in 1960 as D286) is seen arriving at Doncaster's Platform 3B on a four-coach cross-country passenger train. The following year, the loco was scrapped at Doncaster Works.

The year 1984 saw the introduction of the Class 141 Pacer diesel multiple units, built by the Leyland National bus factory in Workington. Brand new at the time, in the summer of 1984, was set No. 141010, sitting in Platform 7 at Doncaster, on a service to Leeds. The unit is painted in West Yorkshire Passenger Transport Executive Metro livery. The Class 141 was not considered a success and this particular one was later exported to Iran.

Test Coach *Iris* was once part of a two-coach Derby Lightweight DMU built in 1954, later transformed into two single cars. It was used for radio survey work and is seen at Doncaster station in the spring of 1986, awaiting the signal out of the siding between Platforms 6 and 7. It has since been restored to passenger carrying condition.

British Railways' D1724 had become No. 47549 when photographed at Doncaster station's Platform 4 in mid-1987. Named *Royal Mail*, the loco is seen in the latest InterCity livery, but is in charge of a Down train of Mk I coaching stock in British Rail blue and grey.

The late 1980s saw electrification reach Doncaster. A total of thirty-one Class 91 locomotives were built at Crewe for use on the East Coast Main Line, in conjunction with rakes of new Mk IV carriages. In the spring of 1989, we see loco No. 91012 with its new rolling stock in the west sidings beside Doncaster station. In one of the adjacent roads is EMU No. 307118. This unit had been built at Eastleigh Works for use on the former Great Eastern Railway's London suburban services. Still lettered for Network South East duties, it would soon be pressed on to local services to Wakefield Westgate and Leeds.

The Class 91 locomotives had two differing cabs. The arrangement is shown in the above photograph, seen in push-pull mode. In the event of the need, the loco could be run around the train and pull the carriages as a normal loco-hauled service. Because the 'blunt end' of the loco was not streamlined, it was restricted to 110 mph. On regular duties, with close coupling to the leading Mk IV carriage, this part of the loco soon became absolutely filthy. It is obvious, therefore, that No. 91003 is brand new when photographed at Doncaster in spring 1989.

Electric locomotive No. 89001 was unique on British Rail metals. It was built as a prototype in 1986, but the rest of the fleet was never ordered. It was used on King's Cross–Leeds services once electrification was complete. It is seen here on such a working while calling at Doncaster's Platform 4 in December 1988. The locomotive was later named *Avocet*. It was withdrawn in 1992, but later reinstated by GNER, before final withdrawal in 2001. It is now in the hands of preservationists.

The early days of the Class 91 locomotives saw numerous failures. One such occurred in February 1992, which resulted in InterCity-liveried No. 31407 propelling the train into Platform 8 at Doncaster station, where the service was terminated. New as D5640 in 1960, No. 31407 lasted until 2006, when it was scrapped.

Electrification of the Doncaster–Leeds line saw the local service converted to EMU operation. Built in the mid-1950s for Great Eastern services out of Liverpool Street, five units were sent up north and painted in West Yorkshire PTE colours. No. 307111 is seen in Platform 6 at Doncaster in 1990, ready for departure. These sets were meant only as a stop-gap and were replaced by new Class 321/9 units in 1993.

Further units from the Eastern Region were also transferred to the Leeds area for newly electrified Aire Valley services from Leeds and Bradford to Skipton and Ilkley. The Class 308 sets were built in the early 1960s for Liverpool Street outer suburban duties, while a further batch was constructed for Fenchurch Street routes out to Tilbury and Southend-on-Sea. Doncaster Works got the job of overhauling a batch of these EMUs, converting them to three-car sets. No. 308163 and a sister are seen at Doncaster, still in Network South East colours in late 1993. New Class 333 units, introduced in 2000, later replaced the 308s.

Right up until the 1990s, Doncaster station had a station pilot locomotive, used for shunting carriages as required. In Railfreight grey is No. 08877, resting between duties at Doncaster in the autumn of 1991. The photograph was taken from the old cattle dock platform, latterly used for car parking. Recent developments on this site have seen the building of the new Platform 0.

This 0-6-0 diesel shunter No. 08500 had received an unofficial number and name, *Thomas No 1*, when photographed in Doncaster's West Sidings in late 1993. Class 08 shunters are still regularly seen in this area, operated by Wabtec and used for shunting rolling stock in and out of that company's works.

In the spring of 1992, with resident shunter No. 08745 in charge of the movement, electric locomotive No. 86612 is being shunted around Doncaster station's west sidings. Named *Elizabeth Garrett Anderson* after the famous pioneering physician and suffragette, it was built in 1965 at Doncaster Works and delivered as E3122 for West Coast Main Line duties. It has just re-emerged from its birthplace, newly repainted into British Rail's Railfreight grey livery.

The late 1980s saw traditional DMUs being replaced by Pacer sets, formed of lightweight four-wheel carriages. In mid-1992, on the right, at Platform 7 at Doncaster station is No. 142004. This unit, built by the Leyland National bus factory at Workington, is seen in Greater Manchester orange livery – well out of its normal territory. In West Yorkshire PTE colours at Platform 6 is No. 144011. The chassis of this unit was built at Derby Works, the body constructed by Scottish bus builder Alexander.

Pacers from other parts of the BR network could be found at Doncaster, en route to and from the Plant. The Class 142 units from the west of England were known as 'Skippers' and painted into an appropriate brown-and-cream colour scheme. They were not successful on the former Great Western Railway branch lines, and so were soon transferred elsewhere. Sometime in 1988, No. 142016 has reached Doncaster and is seen residing in the west sidings.

British Rail's Sprinter Class 150 DMU sets were also used in the Doncaster area. The first production batch, classified as Class 150/1, was built in 1985/6. No. 150111 is seen during one evening in December 1990 calling at Doncaster's Platform 3B, forming a local service to Sheffield.

The original Class 150 Sprinter was followed, in the late 1980s, by the 156 Super Sprinter units, intended for medium-distance cross-country duties. At Doncaster station, making use of the bi-directional facilities in Platform 4, is No. 156484, one evening in spring 1995. The DMU is seen in the livery applied when it was new.

Following the delivery of General Motors-built Class 59 locos to Foster Yeoman and Amey Roadstone for heavy aggregate work from quarries in Southern England, National Power decided to adopt the same policy for coal traffic to their northern power station. Six locomotives in total were received, based at a new depot at Ferrybridge, West Yorkshire. The first one delivered, No. 59201 *Vale of York*, is seen heading north through Doncaster in late 1994. National Power sold their operations to English, Welsh and Scottish Railways (EWS) in 1998. The Yorkshire-based Class 59 locomotives were then transferred to duties in the south of England.

British Railways diesel D8083 was built by Robert Stephenson and Hawthorn in Darlington in 1961. Renumbering in the early 1970s saw it become No. 20083, but in 1989 it was allocated number 20903 and given the name *Alison*, with Hunslet-Barclay livery, for use on the weed-killing train. On a foggy day in the autumn of 1992, it is seen in the west sidings at Doncaster. The loco later came into the hands of Direct Rail Services; this period including a trip to Kosovo. It is now preserved on the Bo'ness & Kinneil Railway in Scotland.

Delivery of British Rail's heavy-duty freight locomotive Class 60 began in 1989. This example, No. 60014, named *Alexander Fleming* after the discoverer of the first antibiotic, was delivered in January 1993. It is seen passing through Doncaster's Platform 3B on an Up steel train in spring 2002. At the time of writing the loco has been placed in storage by DB Schenker.

The movement of mail and parcels by rail is now almost a thing of the past, but British Rail considered that it had a bright future. Consequently Rail Express Systems (RES) was formed in the early 1990s. Painted in that sector's red livery is electric loco No. 90019, named *Penny Black*, on a Down mail service at Doncaster station's Platform 4 in the summer of 1994. Built in 1989 for West Coast Mail Line duties, this loco received its name in 1990 and would later be painted in First Scotrail colours.

Another RES locomotive, No. 47737 *Resurgent*, is seen alongside Doncaster station in December 2002. It is on standby duties in case of the failure of a Class 91 or the overhead lines on the East Coast Main Line, both of which were not too infrequent in the early days of electrification. Many RES locomotives received names beginning with those three letters. This particular one was new in 1965 as D1773, later to become No. 47178 and then No. 47588, before receiving its last number in 1995. The locomotive was scrapped around 2008. The Class 47 locos used for emergency duties were later replaced by Class 67 diesels (often nicknamed 'Thunderbirds'), a situation remaining in 2017.

Rail Express Systems Class 47 locomotives were often used on rail tour duties towards the end of their lives. On 29 June 2002, No. 47791 is seen at Platform 4 at Doncaster with a northbound special formed of privately owned Mk I and II coaching stock. The tour had started at Stevenage and was destined for Edinburgh, via the scenic Settle and Carlisle route. No. 47791 was new as D1969 in 1965 and lasted until 2013 when it was sold for scrap to C. F. Booth of Rotherham.

'LoadHaul' was the name given in 1994 by British Rail to its northern area freight-operating sector in the run-up to privatisation. The original proposal was for each of these businesses to be sold off separately but, in the event, LoadHaul was purchased in 1996 by EWS, along with sister companies Mainline and Transrail. In the spring of 2002, Doncaster-built No. 56107 is seen passing through Doncaster station with a short Up steel working. Owned by EWS, it still bears its LoadHaul livery. It never received EWS colours and was withdrawn in 2010, being sold for scrap a year later.

English Welsh and Scottish Railway painted its locomotives in a pleasant red-and-yellow colour scheme, similar to that of its associated business in the United States, Wisconsin Central. Seen in that livery is an unusual visitor to Doncaster station, No. 86261. Named *The Rail Charter Partnership*, it is seen in the berthing siding between Platforms 6 and 7 in late 1999. New as E3118 in 1965, being built at Doncaster Works, it met its final demise in South Yorkshire, as it was scrapped at Booth-Roe Metals in Rotherham after withdrawal in 2004.

Another loco built at the Plant was No. 58016, new in 1984. In this photograph, taken in 1996, it has just paid another visit to the works, where it had received an overhaul and EWS livery. Looking very smart, it is seen in Doncaster station's west sidings, ready to depart with the Doncaster Works ABB test train.

Very much the standard EWS coal train at the time of the spring of 2002, EWS No. 66237 is at the head of a rake of HAA merry-go-round wagons. It is heading south along the Up main through Doncaster station. Despite the modernity of the photograph, there are several features shown that have now disappeared. The multi-storey car park in the middle background has been replaced by the new Frenchgate Centre; four-wheel HAA wagons have been replaced by new bogie cars; while No. 66237 has since been transferred to Poland. The loco had been built in 2000 at London, Ontario, Canada.

Commencing in 1997, MTL was awarded the franchise to operate the former Regional Railways North East local services. Later that year, a rebranding exercise saw a new livery introduced, with Northern Spirit becoming the title of the operation. On a sunny spring day in 2000 the new colours are seen to good effect on DMU Super Sprinter No. 156484, photographed at Platform 7 at Doncaster.

In 2000 MTL, the operator of local trains around Doncaster, was purchased by Arriva, with the franchise being rebranded as Arriva Trains Northern the following year. DMU No. 150272 is seen at Platform 3B at Doncaster on a stopping service to Sheffield in the spring of 2002. The unit, though branded for Arriva, still carries its old Regional Railways livery.

British Rail ordered a batch of Class 155 two-car Sprinter DMU sets from British Leyland at Workington. They were delivered during 1987 and 1988. Not long after, BR realised that they had a need for a single car DMU for use on some rural routes. The solution was provided by splitting up the Class 155 units into two Class 153 single cars, putting an extra driving cab in each one. Newly painted in Arriva Trains Northern colours is No. 153328 in July 2002, just terminated in Platform 7 at Doncaster.

Delivery of the Class 158 DMU sets to British Rail's Provincial Sector began in 1989. These were intended for the cross-country express routes that did not justify longer trains. One such duty was the Cleethorpes–Manchester service in the hands of Northern Spirit and, later, Arriva Trains Northern. Arriving at Doncaster on such a working in May 2001, in its dedicated 'Transpennine' livery, is No. 158767. It will use Platform 3B, then cross the layout to get to the Sheffield line.

The occasional steam-operated special train can still be seen at Doncaster, usually bringing out crowds of interested people. However, the first day of October 2005 seems to have been an exception as Platform 4 appears devoid of the human race! The steam loco is former London Midland & Scottish Railway 4-6-2 No. 6233 *Duchess of Sutherland*, which hauled the train up to the Newcastle area for a tour of the freight lines around Bedlington.

On privatisation, the franchise to operate the service from London St Pancras to Nottingham and Sheffield, with occasional forays to Leeds, York and beyond, was awarded to Midland Mainline, a subsidiary of National Express. This HST, with power car No. 43049 trailing, has just come off the Sheffield line and is standing in Platform 4 at Doncaster in mid-2002.

Midland Mainline also received a batch of Class 222 express diesel multiple units, partly to release the HST sets to other duties on the network. Similar to the Voyagers of Virgin Trains, the 222s came in four-, five- and seven-car formations. An unidentified one of the former is seen in Platform 4 at Doncaster, about to depart for Scarborough via York on 1 October 2005. The Midland Mainline franchise later went to East Midlands Trains, part of the Stagecoach Group, and that company's units still make an appearance at Doncaster, including the direct service to Lincoln.

The Class 221 five-car Super Voyager was introduced during the first two years of the twenty-first century for Virgin Trains West Coast Main Line and CrossCountry services. On one of the latter duties in March 2003, set No. 221105 calls at Doncaster before heading north to Newcastle. It will be able to exploit its maximum speed of 125 mph, but the tilting facility will not be available. The CrossCountry franchise has since been awarded to Arriva.

Great North Eastern Railway (GNER), owned by Bermudan company Sea Containers, was awarded the franchise to run the intercity services on the East Coast Main Line and its important branches. A striking dark-blue livery was applied to the fleet of Class 91 electric locos and Mk IV coaches, plus the famous High Speed Trains. One of these is seen departing from Platform 3 at Doncaster, heading for London King's Cross in summer 2001. A Class 142 Pacer sits in the little-used Platform 2.

Dissatisfied with the performance of the Class 91 electric locomotives, GNER had them rebuilt to become Class 91/1, with appropriate renumbering. Newly out-shopped No. 91101 stands at Platform 4 at Doncaster while in charge of a northbound express in spring 2000.

With only one GNER train per day serving the city of Kingston-upon-Hull, GB Railways and their partners Renaissance Railways saw a gap in the market for an 'open access' operation between London King's Cross and Hull. Trains began running in September 2000, using Class 170 Turbostar DMU sets on hire from Anglia Railways, a GB Railways-owned franchise. No. 170204 is seen arriving at Doncaster, Platform 4, in summer 2001. Upon departure it will proceed northwards to Selby, then head for Brough and Hull. The 170s were later replaced by four-car Class 222 Pioneer sets.

First Group later took over the Hull Trains operations, replacing the Class 222 units with Class 180 Adelante sets transferred from Great Western duties. On a snowy 4 December 2010, a late-running King's Cross–Hull working formed of unit No. 180109 is seen arriving at Doncaster, about to cross from the Down main to Platform 3B.

It was not only EWS who purchased Class 66 locomotives for their freight operations. GB Railfreight (GBRF) was founded in 1999, unlike its competitors EWS and Freightliner, who had inherited former British Rail sectors. GBRF-owned No. 66703 is seen running light through Doncaster station in summer 2002. Class 66 locos are still a common sight on freight workings around Doncaster.

When BR steam ended in 1968, who would have thought that the twenty-first century would see a brand new steam locomotive running on the national rail network? On 18 April 2009 Class A1 4-6-2 No. 60163 *Tornado*, first steamed in 2008, is seen passing through Doncaster at speed on the return working from York with the 'Yorkshire Pullman' tour. Earlier that day, No. 60163 had made its first departure from London's King's Cross station.

Most of Virgin's CrossCountry franchise transferred to Arriva in 2007, including the South West to North East services passing through Doncaster. A new livery was soon applied to the Class 220 and 221 Voyager fleet. On 28 June 2008, No. 220008 calls at Platform 4 on its northbound journey.

Following the collapse of the GNER East Coast franchise, National Express took over. However, that company too ran into difficulties and in November 2009 East Coast Trains, a subsidiary of the government-owned Directly Operated Railways, began running the services. Saturday 10 December 2010 saw Doncaster's rail services disrupted by poor weather, with East Coast Trains No. 91107 running 'blunt-end' first at the south end of a 225 set. The loco has received its East Coast colours, but the rest of the train is still in GNER blue.

As well as the company's Class 66 fleet, Freightliner bought a batch of Class 70 locomotives, built by General Motors in Erie, Pennsylvania. Number 70017, built in 2012, is seen by itself at Doncaster station on 10 April 2015. In all, twenty locomotives were received by Freightliner, with Colas Rail also buying a further ten.

December 2004 saw the Northern Rail franchise awarded to Serco-Abellio, who took over operations from Arriva Trains Northern and First North Western, covering all local services in Northern England. Pacer unit No. 144005 is seen in its Northern Rail colours arriving at Doncaster on a service from Goole or Scunthorpe on 18 April 2009. The franchise has since transferred to Arriva.

Coaching stock and multiple units from other franchises are often seen at Doncaster, before or after visiting the Wabtec works. On 3 March 2016, EMU No. 321417 is seen in the station's west sidings, showing off its newly applied London Midland colour scheme.

2016 saw the construction of a new Platform 0, situated next to the new Frenchgate Centre, but with access only by a new footbridge from the main Up side island platform. The reason for its construction is to provide a terminating point for local trains from the Thorne direction, thus freeing up Platforms 1 and 3, which are intensively used by through services. On 2 November 2016, the work neared completion.

Also on 2 November 2016 an Up HST in Virgin Trains East Coast livery passes through Doncaster at speed on the Up fast line. The leading power car is No. 43274, named *Spirit of Sunderland*. Virgin Trains East Coast took over the franchise on 1 March 2015 and soon began painting its fleet in this smart colour scheme.

Doncaster Works (The Plant)

Doncastrians have always referred to the town's railway works as the 'Plant', where many of Britain's steam locomotives were built and maintained. Perhaps one of the most famous of those was *Flying Scotsman*, an A3 class 4-6-2 Pacific. After a lifetime of front-line operations on the East Coast Main Line, the loco was withdrawn in 1963. It was saved from the scrapyard by a Doncaster businessman, Alan Pegler, who gained an agreement with British Railways to operate the loco on BR metals. Mr Pegler had *Flying Scotsman* repainted into LNER colours and it regained its old number, 4472. In 1969, it was decided that the loco would tour the United States. Therefore *Flying Scotsman* revisited the Plant for adaptations prior to operating on USA railroads. Here is the loco in the Plant yard, in that year, fitted with its double tender, US-style whistle, bell and cowcatcher (correctly called a 'pilot').

After the end of steam, locomotive construction continued at the Plant. British Rail's second batch of Class 56 diesels was built in the works. Brand new in 1980, No. 56084 looks smart in its 'large logo' BR corporate livery, seen from the main works entrance in Hexthorpe. No. 56084 had a short life and was sold for scrap in 2009.

Many of British Rail's Eastern Region-allocated locomotives were sent to the Plant for major overhauls. In addition, BR's Class 50 diesels, operating on the Western Region, were refurbished at Doncaster during the late 1970s and early 1980s. During an open day at the Plant in June 1978, No. 50021 is on display, newly painted in all-over blue. Built by English Electric as D421 in 1968 for West Coast Main Line operations, the loco has since been preserved.

Another Class 50 (No. 50002, named *Superb*) is seen at the Plant during the late 1970s in the company of two Class 03 diesel shunters. The closest is No. 03029, which had been built at BR's Swindon Works in 1958 as number D2029. This particular loco was withdrawn and later scrapped at Doncaster Works in 1979, and so it is assumed that this is the approximate date of the photograph.

Saturday 18 June 1978 was the occasion of an open day at the Plant, with several appropriate
steam engines on display. The oldest of these was Great Northern Railway No. 1, the Patrick
Stirling-designed 4-2-2, built at this location in 1870. The loco normally resides in the National
Railway Museum at York.

One of the most famous steam locomotives was also to be found in the yard outside the Paint
Shop. LNER class A4 4-6-2 No. 4468 *Mallard* had been constructed in the Plant in 1938 and
achieved fame in that year by becoming the fastest steam loco in the world, reaching 125.88 miles
per hour on Stoke Bank near Grantham. That record still stands today. No. 4468 still sees forays
onto the national network and is in the custody of the National Railway Museum.

As well as being known as a place where locomotives were built, Doncaster Works was also where many met their demise, with an area being devoted to cutting up those whose life had come to an end. Such a fate befell Deltic No. 55001 in 1980, here looking very sorry for itself. Just under twenty years earlier, it had been new at English Electric's Vulcan Works at Newton-le-Willows. Latterly it had been named *St Paddy* after the winner of the Epsom Derby and St Leger horse races.

The last Class 55 Deltics were withdrawn in January 1982, with many gaining an appointment with the cutter's torch at the Plant around that period. A line of withdrawn locomotives in the works yard makes a sad sight in that month. Many were to remain here for over a year. Fortunately, a total of six were saved for preservation.

The Plant's Paint Shop was situated just to the right of the main entrance in Hexthorpe. A visit to the Works in 1986 found an unidentified Class 31 ready for its new colours, while in the background a Class 56 freight loco and a Class 50 passenger engine look almost complete.

Most of the heavy repairs and locomotive building took place in the main building at the Plant, known as the Crimpsall or Main Erecting Shops. Fifty Class 58 locomotives were built here between 1983 and 1987. One of the class is not far off completion here when photographed in 1986. It turned out that the Class 58 was the last batch of locomotives to be built at Doncaster Works. The entire fleet had been withdrawn by 2002, though some saw additional service in Europe.

Diesel Multiple Units were maintained and refurbished in their own facility inside the works complex and here in 1986 is DMU car number M51849 lifted up on blocks. This Derby-built Driving Motor Brake Second later became part of BR's Class 115 sets, used around the Merseyside and North West area.

As well as scheduled overhauls, locomotives that had been involved in derailments and collisions were sent to the Plant for repair. Sometime around 1986 No. 37157, based at Eastfield in Glasgow, had been in close contact with something big and heavy. It is seen at the Plant in that year and would later emerge in brand-new condition as No. 37695. Having been new as D6857 in 1963, it had a long life, not being finally withdrawn until 2008.

The Class 08 diesel shunter has long been a feature of the yards within the Plant complex. During a weekend in 1986, No. 08331 is seen there, at its usual berthing point. New as D3401 from BR's Derby Works in 1957, this locomotive saw quite a bit of service around Doncaster Works, but has now passed into preservation.

With the sale of part of the Plant to RFS Industries of Kilnhurst, No. 08331 passed to that business. The loco was later repainted in RFS colours and lost its BR number. However, it gained the name *Terence* and, as such, in the spring of 1989 is seen at the north end of the RFS yard at Doncaster. RFS Industries was later renamed Wabtec Rail Limited and the company still operates ex-BR Class 08 locomotives around what remains of Doncaster Works.

South from Doncaster

The 1947 resignalling of Doncaster station saw Bridge Junction signal box become the first such structure encountered by any southbound train. Situated beside Balby Bridge, it controlled the junction with the curve around to St James Junction on the former GCR Sheffield line. A typical Great Northern Railway design, it is seen here in September 1969 from a southbound passenger train. Like all the boxes in the area, it closed during the 1979 resignalling.

Passing under Balby Bridge, the next signal box to be seen was Sandbank, controlling only the freight lines. Another box of Great Northern Railway design, it was photographed from a southbound passenger train diverted over the goods lines due to engineering work, September 1969.

The two lighting columns seen in the last picture are still in this photograph taken in spring 1980. Sandbank signal box, once situated on what is seen here as a raised grassy area, has now gone, as have the associated sidings. Seen from Balby Bridge, an InterCity 125 heads south towards London. Doncaster Traction maintenance depot (TMD), the former steam shed, can be seen in the left background. The grassed area is today covered with trees and scrub, hiding the TMD site from the view of passengers on the East Coast Main Line.

In the spring of 1970, at Doncaster TMD, Brush Type 4 No. 1543 (later renumbered as 47014), still in green, is seen in the company of two Class 03 locomotives, Nos 2026 and 2137, with newly applied blue paintwork. Both of the diesel shunters survived the renumbering, becoming Nos 03026 and 03137 respectively. No. 2026 was cut up at Booth's scrapyard in Rotherham in 1984, while No. 2137 suffered the same fate at Doncaster Works in 1977.

The familiar sight of Doncaster's steam loco shed (commonly called 'Carr Loco'), adapted for diesel use, forms the backdrop of this photograph of No. 47379 sometime around 1978. Built by Brush Traction at Loughborough in 1965 as number D1898, the loco later joined the Railfreight Sector before its withdrawal in 1999. It was cut up at Wigan Springs Branch TMD. Interestingly, behind the locomotive is a single-car DMU in departmental service, probably in use for 'route learning' driver training.

A final look at Doncaster TMD, as seen in autumn 1980. Resting in the yard outside are the usual Class 08, 31 and 37 locomotives. Accompanying them is a more unusual visitor, a Hudswell Clarke 0-4-0 diesel shunter owned by the National Coal Board, presumably here for an overhaul. The former steam shed, albeit much reduced in size, passed to EWS and remained in use until final demolition. The site will soon be used by Hitachi for the maintenance of their Azuma fleet.

The area alongside and to the south of Doncaster TMD was given over to the vast Decoy, Carr and Belmont freight yards. These are still very much in use today, but not on the same scale as the 1960s. Here, in June 1967, at what is now Belmont Yard, is a regular visitor from the Southern Region, D6571. This was, almost certainly, in charge of an Uddingston (Scotland) to Cliffe (Kent) cement train. The loco later became No. 33053. In the very top background can be seen the former GNR wagon works. (Alan Walker)

Seen in September 1969, Decoy No. 1 was one of many ex-Great Northern Railway signal boxes that once controlled the yards and main lines to the south of Doncaster. Ten years later would see them all rendered redundant with the opening of the new Doncaster Power Signal Box.

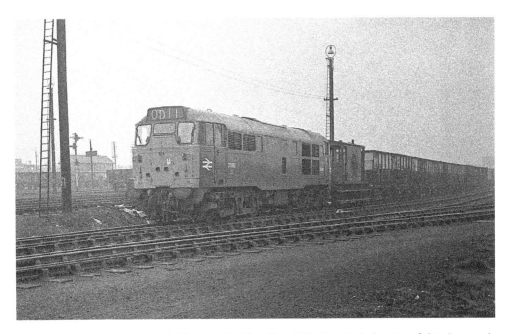

The south end of Decoy Yard, on the Up side of the East Coast Main Line, is the location of this photograph, taken *c.* 1969. Brush Type 2 D5862 is in charge of an empty train of coal hopper wagons, probably destined for one of the local collieries. D5862 later became No. 31327.

Believe it or not, this is almost the same location as the top photograph, albeit taken from the A618 White Rose Way road bridge, built in the 1980s. What was once marshy wasteland in the right background is now covered by vast industrial buildings, forming part of the Doncaster Railport complex. This is served by a container terminal, reached by the single-track connection passing through the gate clearly seen. GBRf Nos 66766 and 66747 are arriving into Decoy sidings to pick up their train on 1 July 2016, while a pair of EWS/DBS Class 66 locos are waiting for the GBRf movement to pass through. Meanwhile, on the Up slow line, a Freightliner Class 66 waits for the signal to clear before heading south.

Viewed from a southbound train diverted over the goods lines in September 1969 is Potteric Carr signal box. The former GNR structure controlled the single line connection to the South Yorkshire Joint Line, which can be seen diverging to the left. This spur joined the SYJR at Low Ellers Junction. It is still in use today.

South of Potteric Carr, the East Coast Main Line passed through the Black Carr area, with its maze of railway lines and wetlands. The map at the front of this publication will give you an idea of the layout in 1967, though it has altered considerably today. At the south end of the complex was Loversall Carr Junction, where the curves from the Dearne Valley line joined the ECML. It is here that we see Brush Type 4 No. 1550, sometime around 1968. It is working northbound with 3Z05, a special empty coaching stock train. No. 1550 was the first of a batch of 202 built at Crewe – the others had been built at Loughborough. The loco later became No. 47435 and was withdrawn in 1993.

The first station on the East Coast Main Line south of Doncaster was situated at Rossington, serving the old village and the newer estates built for the adjacent colliery. Never able to compete with the frequent bus service, it closed as early as 1958. Nevertheless it remained intact until the 1960s. The northbound platform is seen, rather overgrown, from an Up express in September 1969. The level crossing today is controlled from Doncaster Power Signal Box, with assistance from CCTV, while the semaphore signals have disappeared too.

Bawtry station was the next one heading south on the Great Northern route to London, serving a small town. Like Rossington it was closed in 1958, though goods and excursion traffic survived a few more years. Seen from the approach road *c.* 1969 are the main station building and the goods shed, on the Down side. Royalty attending the St Leger race meeting often alighted here, using road transport onwards, rather than face the crowds and heavy traffic in central Doncaster. Bawtry was also the junction for the Tickhill Light Railway, built by the GNR, which never served Tickhill, but was used by freight to Misson until the mid-1960s.

The former Great Northern and Great Eastern Joint line left the GNR main line at Black Carr Junction, forming the route towards Lincoln and a diversionary route to Huntingdon. The first signal box south of Black Carr was at Bessacarr, where the easternmost spurs from the Dearne Valley Railway came in, the southbound one crossing the girder bridge in the background. At the time of this photograph, the exit from that spur was still controlled by an ex-GNR somersault signal. About to pass the signal box and its associated level crossing is a short Up freight, with Brush Type 2 D5802 and an unidentified English Electric Type 3 providing more than adequate motive power, *c.* 1969.

Around the same time as the above photograph, an early British Rail tamping machine is seen at Bessacarr, presumably off to carry out duties on the Up line a few hundred yards ahead, as indicated by the temporary speed restriction warning board.

The GN & GE Joint passes beside the new Robin Hood Airport, but no station has yet been built to serve it. Prior to its conversion to civil use, the airfield was RAF Finningley, hosting part of Britain's 'V Bomber' strategic nuclear strike force. Every September the gates were thrown open to the public for the base's 'At Home' day, which caused chaos to the local road system. An attempt to alleviate this was the building of a temporary platform beside the airfield, on the Down line only. A frequent service was operated from Doncaster, formed of DMU sets, passing by southwards, before reversing at Finningley signal box. On 19 September 1981 a six-car set is about to depart empty for Doncaster, where it will pick up another load of eager passengers.

The first passenger station heading south on the GN & GE Joint was at Finningley, which lost its regular services in 1961. However, the station remains remarkably intact when photographed in 1979, looking south from the level crossing and signal box of GNR design.

North from Doncaster

North of Doncaster station the railway splits into three routes: east towards Thorne, Hull and Grimsby, north to York and northeast in the direction of Wakefield and Leeds. Approaching Doncaster at Marshgate Junction is West Yorkshire PTE Metro-liveried EMU No. 321901 of Northern Rail on 5 September 2009. This is nearing the end of its all-stations service from Leeds. To the right is a series of grey buildings, on the site of Marshgate goods depot, accessed from the Great Central line. The background is dominated by St Georges Bridge, opened in 2001, carrying the new main road northwards and relieving congestion on North Bridge, from where this photograph was taken.

Continuing north on the ECML, the first signal box was at Arksey, a Great Northern Railway structure. The station here closed to passengers on 5 August 1952, but the signal box remained to control the level crossing, as seen *c.* 1969. After resignalling, the box was demolished in 1980, with the crossing controlled by CCTV and lifting barriers.

North of Arksey, the ex-Lancashire & Yorkshire Railway line to Askern and Knottingley leaves the ECML at Shaftholme Junction. Just to the north of that, the main line passed under the Stainforth–Adwick line, with a curve coming round to Joan Croft Junction. It is here, on 1 July 2016, that we see a First Hull Trains Class 180 DMU heading for Selby and beyond. The whole layout is crossed by the new bridge connecting the line from Stainforth with the Askern route. This opened in 2014 and enabled heavy freight trains to avoid using the busy ECML.

The Shaftholme Junction–Knottingley line passes through the centre of the small town of Askern, once famous for its spa waters, but latterly known for its colliery and associated coking plant. The level crossing was controlled by this mechanical signal box of Lancashire & Yorkshire Railway design. It is seen still in use in early 1980, not long before closure in October of that year.

Askern station closed to passengers as early as 1948, but remained intact for excursion traffic until the 1960s. The line is often used by diverted passenger trains, such as this Up HST led by power car No. 43118, seen passing through the remains of the platforms in 1982. The train had been sent via Askern due to ongoing work constructing the Selby Diversion of the ECML, which opened a year later. Today passenger trains once again traverse the line as Grand Central send some of their West Yorkshire services that way, but Askern station has not reopened, despite various calls from pressure groups.

The National Coal Board had a considerable rail network serving their facilities at Askern. Steam traction, in the form of a Hunslet Austerity 0-6-0ST, survived into the 1970s. However the diesel fleet was quite interesting, including an ex-British Railways Barclay 0-6-0 and this loco, No. 45. Seen outside the engine shed, *c.* 1977, it is a 1956-built Ruston 0-6-0, works number 384146. The colliery closed in 1985.

The West Riding and Grimsby Joint Line

The West Riding & Grimsby Railway was jointly owned by the Great Northern and Great Central Railways until the 1923 Grouping. The route consisted of the Doncaster–Wakefield Westgate line, still open to passengers, plus the freight-only Adwick–Stainforth section. Coming out of Doncaster, the first signal box encountered was Bentley Crossing, a GNR design, seen from a passing train in 1969. The box survived until 1980.

It is believed that there was once a miner's platform beside Bentley Crossing, but it was not until 1992 that a public station opened. Today trains call twice hourly on weekdays. A few weeks after the station began life, Barclay-Alexander three-car Pacer unit No. 144020 departs for Adwick. The following train northwards will be an EMU forming the all-stations service to Leeds.

At the next signal box along the WR&G, Castle Hills Junction, the branch from Brodsworth Colliery met the main line. Originally there had been only a north-facing junction, but alterations brought in on 14 September 1969 saw the commissioning of a triangular layout, while the sidings and signal box were abolished, with control passing to Carcroft station signal box. The new south–west chord at Castle Hills Junction is seen under construction earlier in 1969.

The construction of Brodsworth Colliery began in 1905 and the first coal was raised three years later. Considerable rail facilities were provided, as can be seen from this 1982 view of the approach to the pit from the Castle Hills Junction direction. By the time of this photograph internal NCB traffic had ceased and the colliery's Barclay diesel shunter was awaiting disposal, as was the fleet of wagons seen. Hidden out of view in the bushes on the right was a brick-built platform, which would once have seen miners boarding their trains home. Brodsworth Colliery was also served by rail from the western side, with a connection to the Hull & Barnsley Railway at Pickburn, though this was removed in 1968.

Carcroft and Adwick-le-Street was, until closure to passengers in 1967, the first stop out of Doncaster for Leeds-bound local trains. The station remained intact when photographed in 1969; indeed the ornate station building survives today as a private house. In this view we are looking north, with Bullcroft Colliery and its spoil heap visible in the background. The original signal box on the end of the Up platform had been converted for other uses after replacement by the later box by the junction beyond.

In the late 1960s the disused goods sidings at Carcroft and Adwick-le-Street were home to this preserved industrial locomotive, while it was being restored by its owner, the late Terry Robinson. New in 1925 as Avonside Engine Co. works number 1908, for a cement works near Buxton, the loco is seen during 1969 in steam for the first time in many years. The loco, now named *Fred*, was later sold and now regularly runs at Stoomcentrum Maldegem, a preserved railway centre in Belgium.

A new station, named 'Adwick', opened on 11 October 1993, just to the south of the site of the old Carcroft and Adwick-le-Street station. It has a manned booking office and extensive 'Park and Ride' facilities. Like Bentley, it has an hourly service to and from Leeds to Doncaster, while an additional train from Doncaster and beyond terminates here, giving the station two trains an hour southwards. On 10 February 2011 Freightliner locomotive No. 66516 is seen passing through on an Up container train.

The WR&G Doncaster Avoiding Line had a triangular junction with the main Leeds–Doncaster line in the Carcroft and Adwick area. No intermediate passenger stations were built, but a goods facility was constructed at Bramwith. Sometime around 1969, an unidentified English Electric Type 3 (class 37) is seen passing the signal box and level crossing, heading west. Despite the lack of stations, the line has seen passenger services, including a Leeds–Cleethorpes direct service, which ceased in 1979. Today it is often used for diversions during engineering work.

The Great Central East of Doncaster

The West Riding & Grimsby Joint joined the Great Central Railway at Stainforth Junction, just to the west of Stainforth and Hatfield station. The facilities here were quite extensive, as seen in this 1969 view, looking east. The station here is still open today, as an unstaffed halt, now named Hatfield and Stainforth and served by two trains an hour on weekdays. The extensive sidings and the station buildings have now largely vanished. Colour lights controlled from Doncaster have replaced the manual signalling. Hatfield Colliery, seen in the left background, closed in 2015, ending coal production in the South Yorkshire coalfield.

The next station westwards was at Barnby Dun, where the island passenger platform lay between the two fast lines, though the original station building survived alongside the eastbound goods line. The station closed in 1967 and is seen here still intact a year later, looking to the east.

In 1991 a new station was opened, less than a mile from the old Barnby Dun facility, but serving the nearby village of Kirk Sandall. On 4 September 2010, Northern Rail's No. 158793 calls on a journey to Bridlington via Hull. The station has no staff, with tickets being issued by the guard, on the twice-hourly service in each direction.

Heading westwards, the next significant point on the four-track former Great Central Railway is Kirk Sandall Junction, where the South Yorkshire Joint line diverges southwards. Until the early 1980s the signalling here was controlled by this classic example of a GCR box. It is being passed by a westbound train of steel empties, headed by a pair of Class 25 diesels, sometime in the early 1970s.

Today Kirk Sandall Junction forms the westernmost point of the four-track section, as can be clearly seen in this photograph taken on 4 September 2010. First TransPennine DMU No. 185142 passes on a Cleethorpes–Manchester Airport working. The South Yorkshire Joint line can be seen leading off to the right. At one time, there was rail access to the extensive Pilkington's Glass Works, but very little remains of that factory, though glass production is still carried out nearby. The new Kirk Sandall station can just be seen in the distance.

At one time, the four-track layout continued westwards to Bentley Junction, where the Doncaster Avoiding Line left the route into Doncaster. Half a mile from Doncaster station (one cannot argue with that sign!) the final ex-Great Central Railway signal box was encountered, named Marshgate Goods and seen from a passing train in 1977. The box was actually of Manchester, Sheffield & Lincolnshire Railway design. It closed in July 1979. As well as controlling access into Marshgate Goods Yard, it supervised operation of the Wheatley Park branch.

Since the late 1960s Marshgate Goods has been used for infrastructure purposes, a function it still fulfils today. Sometime around 1969, it was home to this fine example of a former Great Central Railway Barnum bogie coach, converted into a mobile workshop for use by the local Signalling and Telegraph Department engineers.

The London & North Eastern Railway built a freight-only branch from Marshgate Goods to the Wheatley Park Industrial Estate, serving various factories on its route of about a mile. En route it crossed the River Don and passed over Milethorne Lane level crossing, before terminating at the International Harvesters factory. No photograph has come to light of a train on the branch (latterly it would have had a Class 08 shunter in charge), but Bob Ashton took this photograph of the entrance to International Harvesters rail sidings just after closure. A small ground frame controlled access. It had been intended to continue the line eastwards to join the South Yorkshire Joint line at Kirk Sandall, but this was never constructed.

The South Yorkshire Joint Line

The South Yorkshire Joint Railway, when built, was owned by five railway companies: the Great Central, the Great Northern, the Lancashire & Yorkshire, the North Eastern, and the Midland. It ran from Kirk Sandall Junction, on the GCR Doncaster–Grimsby line, to Brancliffe Junction near Worksop. Constructed primarily to serve various collieries, it is still in use today, though all the pits have closed. At the northern end of the line, in 1969 a new connection was laid from Kirk Sandall Junction to serve the newly constructed Rockware Glass factory. It is here, *circa* 1972, that we see Brush Type 2 No. 5834 ready to depart. At the time of writing, Rockware (now known as 'Ardagh Glass') still use rail for their deliveries of sand.

Heading south from Kirk Sandall Junction, the first colliery reached was Markham Main, in the Doncaster suburb of Armthorpe. Extensive sidings were laid here, which are being passed by an unidentified Brush Type 2 on a southbound empty mineral train. In a complete contrast to the grimy industrial scene on the right, to the left is a local beauty spot known as Sandall Beat Wood.

The National Coal Board at Markham Main had quite a large internal rail system, with its own locomotives. Steam lasted until 1976, when Hunslet 0-6-0ST (built in 1953) *Arthur* was withdrawn. It later passed into preservation at the Buckingham Railway Centre. A sister loco, presumed to be works number 2688 of 1943, as it is without nameplates, is seen shunting at the pit in 1970. When *Arthur* was rebuilt in 1972, parts from 2688 were used in its reconstruction. (Les Flint)

The signal box controlling access to Markham Main Colliery was known as Markham Sidings, constructed by the LNER, but to Great Central design, as were the signals themselves. In this 1969 photograph, looking north, the running line signals have been converted to upper quadrant, but the signal on the right, controlling egress from the headshunt, is still of GCR design. All signalling has now gone, but the single line through the site remains in use. The colliery closed in 1996.

Propelling movements of considerable distances were commonplace on freight lines in the Doncaster area. Here, in 1969, Brush Type 2 D5839 is at the rear of a trainload of coal from Markham Main Colliery and is heading for Low Ellers Junction, where it will reverse and head into Decoy Yards. It is seen passing Doncaster Airport, which is behind the embankment, to the west side of the former Great North Road.

At Low Ellers Junction, the track doubled over the short section to St Catherine's Junction. Low Ellers was the point where the single-track connection from Potteric Carr came in, as seen in this view looking north in 1978, taken from the bridge crossing over the East Coast Main Line. The sparse passenger service from Doncaster to Shireoaks/Worksop would have used the line to the left, but this ceased operation as early as 1929. Low Ellers Junction signal box did not survive the Doncaster area resignalling.

The Black Carr area saw considerable remodelling in 1977 in preparation for the resignalling project, with new spurs being built over former Dearne Valley Railway land, including new connections to the South Yorkshire Joint line. November 1978 saw English Electric Type 3 No. 37160 suffer a derailment on one of these connecting lines. It is seen from the SYJR line, having just been righted. Having landed in marshy ground, the locomotive sustained little damage and survived until withdrawal in 1993.

At the south end of the double-track section was St Catherine's Junction, controlled by a fine GCR-designed signal box, as seen in this 1969 photograph. We are looking north along the SYJR, with the double-track curve to Black Carr Sidings West leaving to the left.

Saturday 1 March 1986 saw the South Yorkshire Joint Line traversed in both direction by enthusiasts' tours. One was named the 'Capital Jointliner', starting from London with No. 47631 in charge. The other, seen here, was the 'Western Jointliner', which came from Cardiff and Bristol. Locomotive No. 47424 was used for the East Midlands and Yorkshire section of the itinerary and is seen here on the single-track section between St Catherine's Junction and Tickhill & Wadworth on the return leg.

On the same day as the above photograph, we see the remains of the northernmost passenger station on the South Yorkshire Joint, Tickhill and Wadworth. Poorly situated for both villages, it saw very little passenger traffic, though freight and the signal box survived until the 1960s. The station building had suffered a fire some time before the date of this picture, but the former stationmaster's house, being some distance away, was unaffected and still inhabited.

The Great Central West of Doncaster

The former Great Central Railway route towards Mexborough leaves the East Coast Main Line as it passes beneath St James' Bridge. Access ramps from the road above led down to the excursion station named, appropriately, St James' Bridge. Originally consisting of two platforms, by 1969 it had been reduced to one, plus a shorter bay, seen occupied by a rake of ex-LNER and LMS coaching stock in 1969. The station was rarely used, except during the famous Leger Race Week in Doncaster held each September.

The multi-storey St James Street flats once again occupy the background, as a Wickham-built DMU, in use as the General Manager's saloon, is stabled in the bay platform at St James' Bridge, *c.* 1968. It is on display to the public, forming part of an exhibition that included the latest Freightliner containers.

The exit lines from St James' Bridge excursion station joined the goods lines curving round from Bridge Junction and the connection from the GCR passenger lines. The area was controlled by this fine ex-Great Northern Railway signal box, seen in 1969, as Brush Type 2 D5562 waits for the road.

The 1979 resignalling saw the connection to the Mexborough line reduced to a single-lead junction layout. Towards the end of the twentieth century, it became obvious that this had been a mistake and was having a serious effect on punctuality. By 2000, when this photograph was taken (from St James Street flats), the decision had been made to re-double the connection and work was well under way. The new westbound line is seen partly on the site of St James' Bridge excursion station, while an engineer's train sits on what was to become the eastbound line. (Jim Sambrooks)

Opposite St James' Bridge excursion station was once the Midland Railway's Cherry Tree goods depot, latterly occupied by a scrap merchant. The signalling was in the hands of this fine former Great Central Railway box, named Cherry Tree Sidings and seen in 1969. The box controlled the passenger lines as far as Hexthorpe Junction.

The scrapyard at Cherry Tree dealt with a lot of rail traffic – but perhaps the establishment was best known for being home to ex-Kirkstall Forge (near Leeds) Hudswell Clarke 0-4-0ST *Henry de Lacy III* during the late 1960s. An attempt to preserve the loco came to nought, so this industrial shunter was cut up just after this photograph was taken in 1969. Fortunately, identical steam engine *Henry de Lacy II* did not meet the same fate and currently resides on the Middleton Railway in Leeds.

Three double-track lines came together at Hexthorpe Junction: the goods lines joined the passenger ones and the GCR Doncaster Avoiding Line came in from the northeast. Passing the ex-GCR signal box is English Electric Type 3 D6798, running westwards light engine. It is about to cross the former Hull & Barnsley and Great Central Joint line, still *in situ* then (1969) in the deep cutting below.

From Hexthorpe Junction the GCR passed through a deep limestone cutting, known locally as 'Kicking Horse Canyon', which was crossed at great height by the Warmsworth to Sprotbrough road. The early 1960s saw another crossing built, as the A1(M) Doncaster Bypass was constructed. At the end of the cutting, the train passenger was confronted with a contrasting vista of the Don Valley on one side and Steetley's vast Dolomite limestone quarry on the other. This was once rail served and had its own little Ruston four-wheel diesel. The sidings were controlled by this lovely little ex-GCR signal box, named Warmsworth, until rail traffic ceased. It is seen *c.* 1969. The quarry is still very much in use today.

After Warmsworth the GCR line passed along the heavily wooded valley side, then crossed the River Don, after which it plunged into the short Conisbrough Tunnel, during which time it passed under the Dearne Valley Railway. In April 1967, Brush Type 4 D1537 is seen heading east into the tunnel with a trainload of 16-ton wagons loaded with coal. (Alan Walker)

From the same spot, but looking in the opposite direction, again in April 1967, a pair of Sulzer Bo-Bo locos (later to become BR Class 25) is in charge of a long eastbound freight as it passes the signals of Cadeby Colliery signal box. The pit here had two rail exits, the other being onto the Hull & Barnsley Railway's Denaby branch. (Alan Walker)

In 1983, diesel loco No. 45015, seen from the banks of the River Don in Conisbrough, passes Cadeby Colliery with a westbound steel working. The locomotive had been new from BR's Derby Works in 1960 and was withdrawn in 1986, the same year that Cadeby Colliery itself closed.

In modern times the first station out of Doncaster on the former GCR line was at Conisbrough, once a substantial affair serving the historic village and castle, plus offering direct foot access to Cadeby Colliery. The station is still open today, but is now unstaffed and the impressive station building, seen here in the spring of 1983, has been demolished, though the station house survives and is privately occupied. A Doncaster-bound DMU is departing.

The Hull & Barnsley Railway Denaby Branch

The Hull & Barnsley Railway once had a single-track branch from the company's main line at Wrangbrook Junction, built mainly to serve Cadeby and Denaby Collieries. For a few years there was even a passenger service from Carlton on the H&B main line to a simple station at Denaby, though this closed as early as 1903! At its southern end, the layout was controlled by this fine H&BR-built signal box, Denaby A, which gave access to Cadeby Colliery. At this point, NCB locomotives had running powers over BR metals, in order to cross the River Don and gain access to the boat staithe on the Sheffield & South Yorkshire Navigation, plus the sidings at Denaby. The photograph was taken *c.* 1968.

Cadeby Colliery had extensive sidings alongside the H&BR Denaby branch, where NCB Andrew Barclay 0-6-0ST No. 15 is seen hard at work in May 1970. Other steam locos here at the time included a Hudswell Clarke 0-6-0T and a Hunslet 'Austerity' 0-6-0ST, while several diesels were also owned. (Alan Walker)

To house the considerable NCB locomotive fleet at Cadeby Colliery, a substantial shed was built, as viewed in this scene *c.* 1968. Resting outside is a Hudswell Clarke 0-6-0 diesel, one of several ordered for use in the South Yorkshire coalfield.

Having parted company with the NCB sidings at Cadeby Colliery, the H&BR Denaby branch passed under the Dearne Valley Railway (which also once had connections to Cadeby and Denaby Collieries) and entered the short Cadeby Tunnel. At the east portal, seen here *c.* 1968, a ground frame gave access to Middleton Sidings, where a Steetley quarry and associated plant were situated. After closure of the rest of the line, the section to Middleton Sidings was retained until traffic ceased in the 1970s.

Cement traffic at Middleton Sidings was shunted by Steetley's own locomotive, a Yorkshire Engine Company 0-4-0 diesel, seen sometime around 1968. It is in charge of a rake of BR flat wagons, each specially designed to carry three containers of cement, a now obsolete means of transportation.

Despite being closed to passengers in 1903, Sprotbrough station remained intact until final closure. The station is seen, looking south, just after closure, *c.* 1967. There was once a passing loop here, controlled by a diminutive signal box, but this was later reduced to a siding, wherein the main goods traffic was loaded into trains from that ugly concrete loading platform partly obscuring the station building. Amazingly, that wooden structure still survives at the time of writing.

The next station along the line was at Pickburn, a few miles to the northeast of Doncaster. Alterations to the track layout, in association with the construction of the H&BR connection into Brodsworth Colliery, meant that most of the platforms were demolished and the original signal box replaced by a standard H&B structure. In this view, looking south in 1968, the demolition train has arrived, with a Fowler diesel of T. W. Ward (Scrap Merchants) in charge. Within hours of this photograph, all rails had been removed, while the station building and signal box were pulled down and burnt.

A mile or so north of Pickburn, the H&BR Denaby branch crossed the WR&G Doncaster–Wakefield line by this substantial girder bridge, seen after closure in 1968. Itself built by the LNER to replace an earlier structure, the bridge was later completely removed, though the concrete piers can still be glimpsed from a passing express below.

The Hull & Barnsley and Great Central Joint Line

Bullcroft Junction was the hub of operations of the HB & GC line. It marked the end of Hull & Barnsley influence and all the signalling southwards was of Great Central Railway manufacture. Bullcroft Junction signal box was built by Saxby and Farmer to a standard H&B design. At the time of this photograph, *c.* 1968, the line north of here was still in use to enable merry-go-round coal trains to serve Thorpe Marsh power station, most of which used the single line spur from Skellow Junction, seen on the right. The double track line to the left, already out of use, went into Bentley Colliery. Beside that was once a two-road engine shed, long since demolished. The main line south is still showing signs of traffic, though very few trains ran this way at the time.

Here is the H&B-designed signal box at Bullcroft Junction, pictured when still in use sometime around 1969. It would soon close after the Thorpe Marsh traffic was diverted over a new spur onto the Stainforth–Skellow line that was constructed adjacent to the power station.

In this photograph Brush Type 4 diesel locomotive D1871 comes off the single line from Skellow at Bullcroft Junction with a loaded train of HAA wagons for Thorpe Marsh power station in 1968. The line northwards was double track, but signalled for both directions. Note the sidings on the right, used for storing crippled wagons, but originally constructed to assist in exchanging traffic between the H&B and the GCR.

Bentley Colliery, like many of the South Yorkshire pits, had spurs to two nearby railways: the East Coast Main Line north of Arksey and the HB & GC at Bullcroft Junction. Between the two was an extensive NCB rail system, including a half-mile line to a landsale yard in Bentley village. Though the outlet to Bullcroft Junction was no longer in use when this photograph was taken *c.* 1968, much of the layout was still in use by internal colliery shunters. A Hunslet-built NCB Austerity 0-6-0ST is seen in charge of a rake of BR 16-ton mineral wagons, with a formerly privately owned wooden wagon in use as a coal tender for the loco.

The HB & GC never saw a passenger train, though one had been intended. The only known such working came in the form of a two-car Derby-built DMU on 5 October 1968. The Railway Correspondence and Travel Society (RCTS) hired this unit to tour various freight lines around Doncaster. Having traversed the single line from Skellow Junction, it is seen performing a rather complicated reversing manoeuvre at Bullcroft Junction as it crosses the rusty rails of the Bentley Colliery spur.

Heading south from Bullcroft Junction, the next significant location on the joint line was Doncaster Junction. Controlled by a Great Central Railway-designed signal box, the layout here was built as a triangle with double track spurs leading to the planned passenger station at Doncaster York Road. Cutbacks in the 1930s saw the southern curve removed and the York Road branch singled. Here is the northern junction around 1969, seen from the York Road line looking north. The railtour in the above picture took this curve and became the only passenger service to Doncaster York Road.

The facilities at Doncaster York Road were quite extensive, as seen in this 1968 photograph. A fully signalled station had originally been built, including a passenger platform with two faces. The signalling disappeared in the 1930s. The site of the platform became part of the yard occupied by Booth's scrapyard, with rail access through the gates seen on the right of this photograph. The goods shed can be seen in the right background. Most of the traffic appears to be scrap, though there was an oil terminal alongside Bentley Road, seen in the left background.

Booth's scrapyard at Doncaster York Road employed a couple of diesel shunters in the late 1960s for internal wagon movements around the yard. Seen awaiting their next duties are examples of Planet and Ruston four-wheel locomotives in 1968. One is tempted to imagine that the remains of the former passenger platform could be found under that pile of scrap on the left.

The RCTS railtour of 5 October 1968 is seen again, on the York Road branch, stopped on the single line, thus avoiding the need to clamp any facing points. The tour participants were allowed to disembark, take photographs and generally wander around. That would not be allowed today!

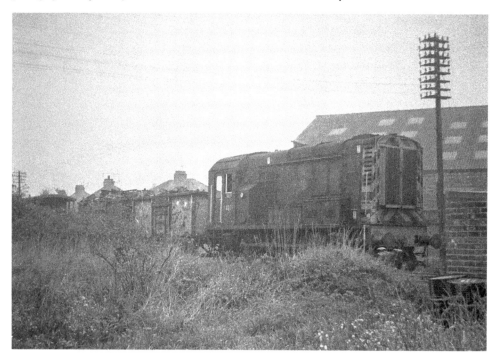

The daily pick-up goods service to York Road was latterly in the hands of a 350-hp diesel shunter. The train is seen here *c.* 1968 with D4078 in charge, which is propelling its short train of scrap past Doncaster Junction signal box on the HB & GC main line. D4078 will remain at the rear through Sprotbrough Junction to Hexthorpe Junction, where it will reverse and head for Hexthorpe Top Yard.

Further towards the south-west, before the joint line went under Sprotbrough Road bridge it passed the four sidings serving the 'Tank Factory'. Access to these was obtained by use of a ground frame released from Sprotbrough Junction signal box, about half a mile to the southwest. At that end of the sidings was a headshunt and a single line leading into the works itself, seen here just before the railway closed in 1969. Opened in 1943 by the Ministry of Supply to manufacture parts for tanks used in the war, the facility retained its nickname throughout its life. The end of hostilities saw the site sold to John Fowler of Leeds, who used it to make steel castings. For internal shunting, a diesel 0-4-0 locomotive was used, manufactured by Fowler's of course. It can just be seen in its brick-built shed, with the rail-mounted steam crane alongside. The whole site has since been cleared and a housing estate built on the land.

Sprotbrough Junction was the point where the HB & GC made double junctions with the former Great Central Railway's Doncaster avoiding line. In this photograph, we are looking east from alongside the joint line, c. 1968. A pair of Brush Type 2 (later known as Class 31) locomotives are passing at speed along the avoiding line with a train of vans for the Humber ports. The leading loco has recently received British Rail's new blue livery, while the other retains its earlier green colours.

Another view of a green-liveried Brush Type 2 at Sprotbrough Junction, sometime around 1968. The train has just come off the HB & GC and consists of coal from Yorkshire Main Colliery and scrap from Warmsworth Junction. The loco is propelling its load over the crossover and up the steep gradient to Hexthorpe Junction, from where it will reverse again and head towards the yards at Doncaster. On freight lines like these, propelling movements were commonplace.

A general view of Sprotbrough Junction, in 1969, seen from the joint line looking west, just after closure of the line to Warmsworth Junction. By this time, the Great Central Railway-designed signal box was only in use when there was traffic for York Road Goods. When this photograph was taken, the box was 'switched out', with the signals in both directions on the avoiding line showing 'off' aspects.

After leaving Sprotbrough Junction, the two lines ran more or less parallel in a southerly direction, though the avoiding line climbed steeply to reach the main GCR route at Hexthorpe Junction. Both lines crossed the River Don at this point. On a foul day in 1968, a Brush Type 4 is in charge of a freight heading towards Mexborough, as it crosses the substantial bridge on the avoiding line. The lower bridge in the background still carried the HB & GC at the time. Beyond that, the pillars of the A1(M) Doncaster bypass can just be seen. All three bridges remain *in situ* at the time of writing, though the middle one now only carries pedestrians and cyclists.

South of Sprotbrough Junction, the HB & GC reached Warmsworth Junction, where it had been intended to build a passenger station. That never happened, but goods facilities were in place, latterly used for scrap traffic. There was also a double-track branch to nearby Yorkshire Main Colliery. Traffic from there was sorted in the sidings to the rear of Warmsworth Junction signal box. The Brush Type 4 seen in this photograph is doing just that as it fly-shunts its brake van into an empty road, prior to picking up another load of coal. The water tower, a relic of steam days, is still *in situ*. The photographer is standing in the space where it had been intended for the northbound passenger platform. The southbound platform would have been opposite.

Here is the GCR-designed signal box at Warmsworth Junction, seen in 1968 looking south. Behind it are the coal sidings, used by traffic from the colliery, while to the extreme right are parts of the scrap yard on the site of the goods depot. Beyond this point, the main line had long been out of use, although officially still open. It had latterly been used for wagon storage.

All rail traffic to Warmsworth Junction ceased in 1969, with Yorkshire Main Colliery being served only by the former Dearne Valley Railway. With closure of its rail facilities, the scrap business here moved elsewhere, leaving the little internal shunting loco with nothing to do. This Ruston four-wheel diesel is seen looking rather forlorn beside the main line in the year of closure. A similar loco remained in use less than a mile away in the extensive quarries alongside the main Doncaster–Sheffield line.

The Dearne Valley Railway

At the meeting point of the 'flying' spurs from Bessacarr Junction on the GN & GE Joint and Loversall Carr Junction on the Great Northern main line was the most easterly signal box on the Dearne Valley Railway, Black Carr Sidings East. It also controlled a long-closed spur to St Catherine's Junction on the South Yorkshire Joint line, plus the LMS connection direct to Rossington Colliery. The latter had closed prior to the period covered by this book. The original structure had been a substantial L&YR box, but was later replaced by the LMS with this one of LNWR design, photographed around 1968.

Not the best of photographs, but an extremely rare one. A 350-hp 0-6-0 diesel shunter is propelling a brake van up the west side spur from the East Coast Main Line at Loversall Carr Junction. It is seen from beside Black Carr Sidings East signal box, under the direction of a fine ex-L&YR lower-quadrant bracket signal. The disused post on this structure once held the signal arm that controlled the vanished spur to St Catherine's Junction on the South Yorkshire Joint line, which can be seen in the right distance. This area was completely remodelled in 1977, as part of the preparations for Doncaster area resignalling.

After Black Carr Sidings West, the line became single track until it reached the next signal box, named 'Yorkshire Main Colliery Sidings Box'. A standard Lancashire & Yorkshire Railway structure, it controlled the DVR's entrance to the main yard serving the pit. It is seen in 1969, looking towards the end of the line at Edlington Halt. The box was later downgraded to a shunter's cabin in 1977, but remained *in situ* until the closure of the line after the colliery succumbed to the same fate.

Around the same time as the above photograph, we see the single-lead entrance/exit from Yorkshire Main Colliery to the Dearne Valley Railway. It looks as though there has been a bit of a shunting problem in the not-too-distant past, involving the trap points and the buffer stop.

Yorkshire Main Colliery, close to the Doncaster suburb of Edlington, had a considerable network of rail sidings, shunted by several NCB locomotives. As late as the last years of the 1960s, steam locomotives were still being used for these duties. Like many collieries in the area, Hunslet Austerity 0-6-0ST engines were employed, but a notable exception was Hudswell Clarke 0-6-0ST No. 18 *Eddie*. Unusually, this loco was purchased second-hand from Appleby-Frodingham steelworks. It is seen, out of use, outside the shed at Yorkshire Main in 1969.

The introduction of merry-go-round operations to collieries in the Yorkshire area meant that the need for NCB internal locomotives was much reduced and they disappeared from most locations. Yorkshire Main Colliery retained this Hunslet 0-4-0 diesel locomotive, seen in the company of two HAA wagons at the pit in spring 1984. The colliery closed the following year.

After closure of the Dearne Valley Railway as a through route in 1966, the line from Yorkshire Main Colliery Sidings signal box to the site of Edlington Halt was retained as a long siding. In 1969, the end of the line is seen, with the wooden fence on the right marking the position of the former rail-level passenger facilities. The former coach body located here was removed shortly after closure of the line's passenger service in 1951. We are looking west, towards Conisbrough Viaduct, with the trackbed passing under the former Hull & Barnsley and Great Central Joint Railway's Yorkshire Main Colliery branch from Warmsworth Junction, which itself closed in 1969.

The Dearne Valley Railway's impressive viaduct over the Don Valley at Conisbrough last saw a train in 1966. However, it remains *in situ*. After a long period of disuse, it is now part of the Sustrans network and is now available to cyclists and walkers, as part of the Trans Pennine Trail.